INSPIRED BY LILY
DEDICATED TO BODHI

Follow us for tips, pep talks and free stuff!

RemixBabyBookSeries   RemixBabyBooks

INFO@REMIXBABYBOOKS.COM   REMIXBABYBOOKS.COM
HARMONYICATPUBLISHING.COM   ISBN: 979-8-9852306-0-4

MILK
open & close fist
a few times

LOOKS LIKE
milking a
cow

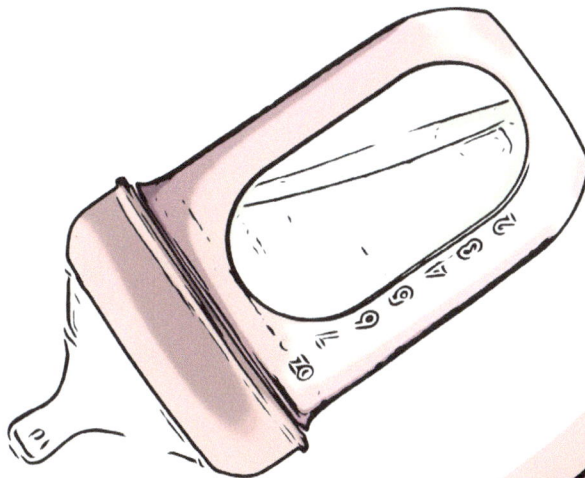

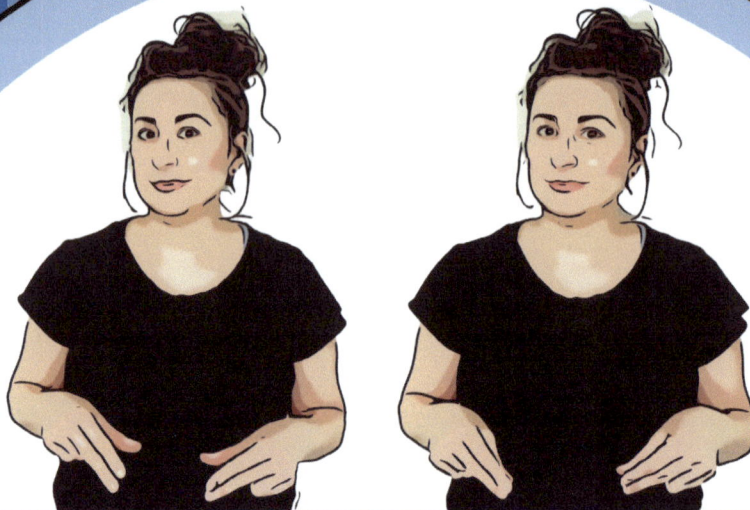

DIAPER
pinch with first
two fingers &
thumb at hip

LOOKS LIKE
pressing
diaper
tabs

CLOTHES
brush down chest with open hands

LOOKS LIKE
dusting off shirt

PLAY
stick out pinkies
& thumbs
then wiggle

LOOKS LIKE
hanging
loose

BALL
curve all fingers then touch hands together

LOOKS LIKE
holding an invisible ball

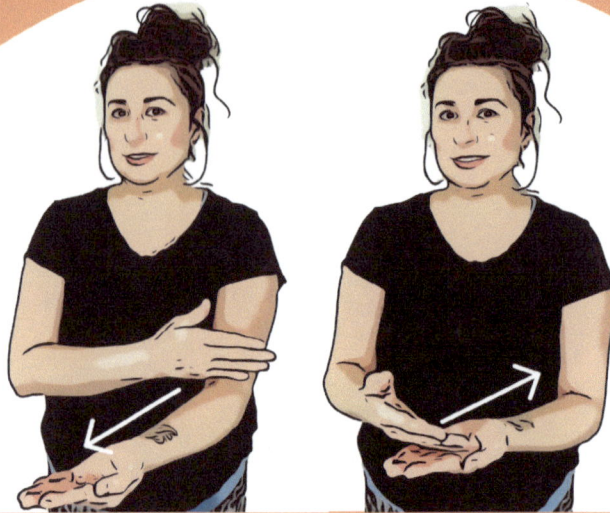

MUSIC
extend forearm
with palm up
then swing flat
hand over arm

LOOKS LIKE
conducting
a choir

BOOK
hold flat hands
with palms
together
then open

LOOKS LIKE
opening
a good
book

CAR
hold fists '10 & 2'
then move
up & down

LOOKS LIKE
holding the
steering
wheel

GENTLE
stroke back of
hand with open
flat hand

LOOKS LIKE
petting a
cute little
animal

CAT
pinch with index
finger & thumb
then pull away
from cheek

LOOKS LIKE
pulling a
whisker

DOG
pat thigh, stick out tongue & pant

LOOKS LIKE
imitating & calling a dog

FOOD
bring fingertips
together
then touch lip

LOOKS LIKE
eating
finger
food

WATER
hold up first three fingers
then tap chin with
index finger

LOOKS LIKE
tapping
W to
chin

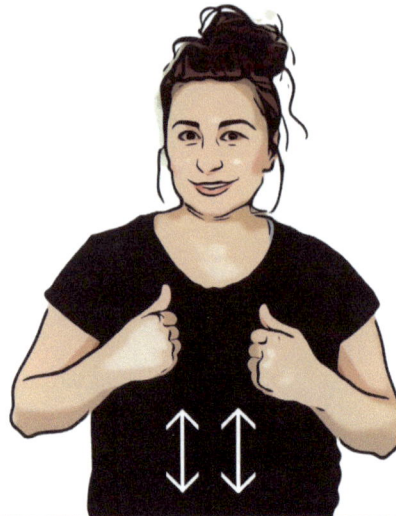

BATH
make fists with
thumbs up
then move up &
down chest

LOOKS LIKE
scrubbing
body in
bath

BED
hold palms together
then rest head
on hands

LOOKS LIKE
sleeping on
prayer
hands

LOVE
make fists
then cross arms
against chest

LOOKS LIKE
crossing
heart

PARENT
open hand
then place thumb
to cheek

LOOKS LIKE
touching five
hand to
cheek

MOTHER
open hand
then tap thumb
to chin

LOOKS LIKE
touching five
hand to
chin

FATHER
open hand
then place thumb
to forehead

LOOKS LIKE
touching
five hand
to fore-
head

BEFORE

MORE   PLEASE

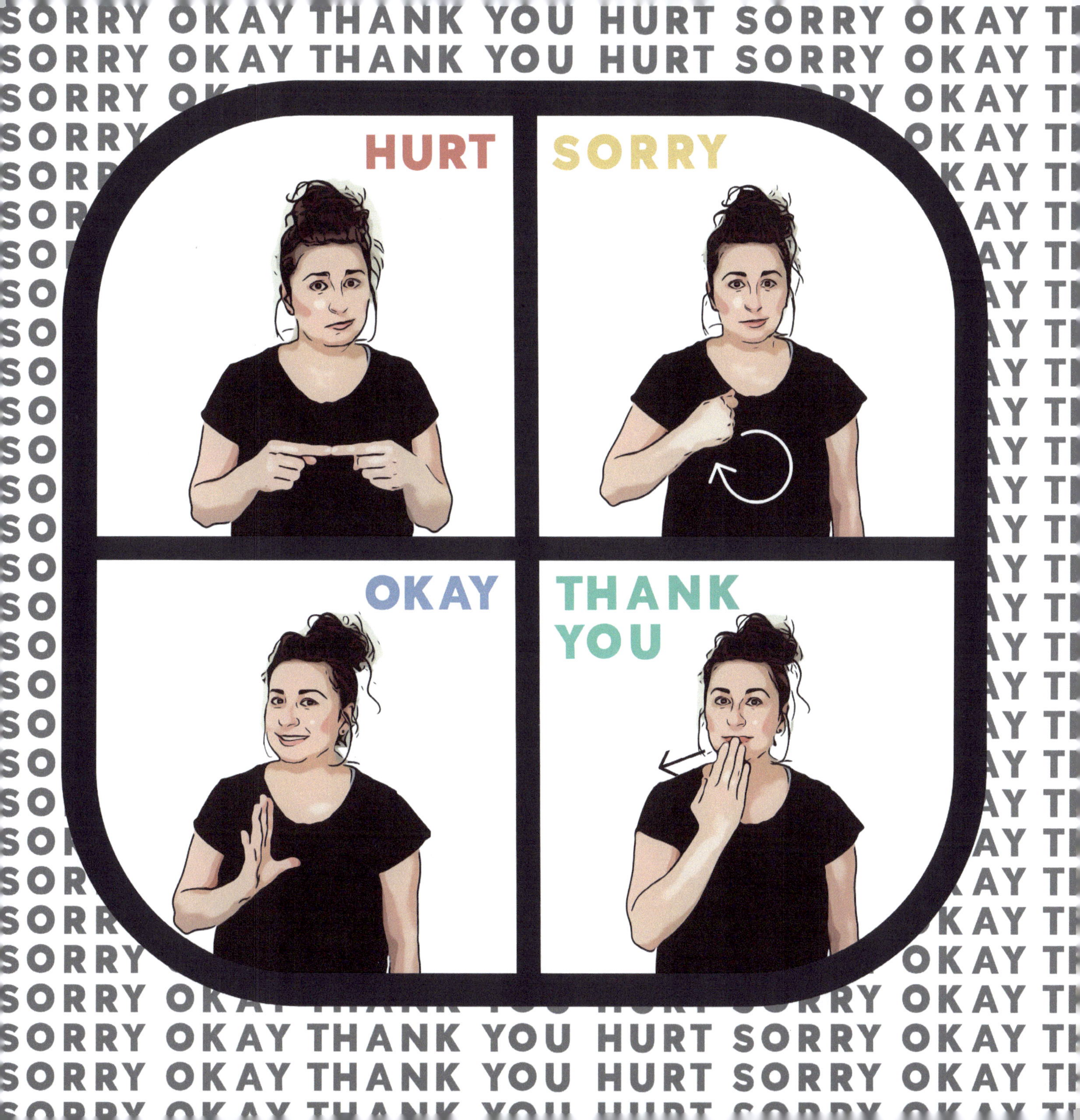
HURT
SORRY
OKAY
THANK YOU

ALL DONE

www.ingramcontent.com/pod-product-compliance
Lightning Source LLC
Chambersburg PA
CBHW042119040426

42449CB00002B/110